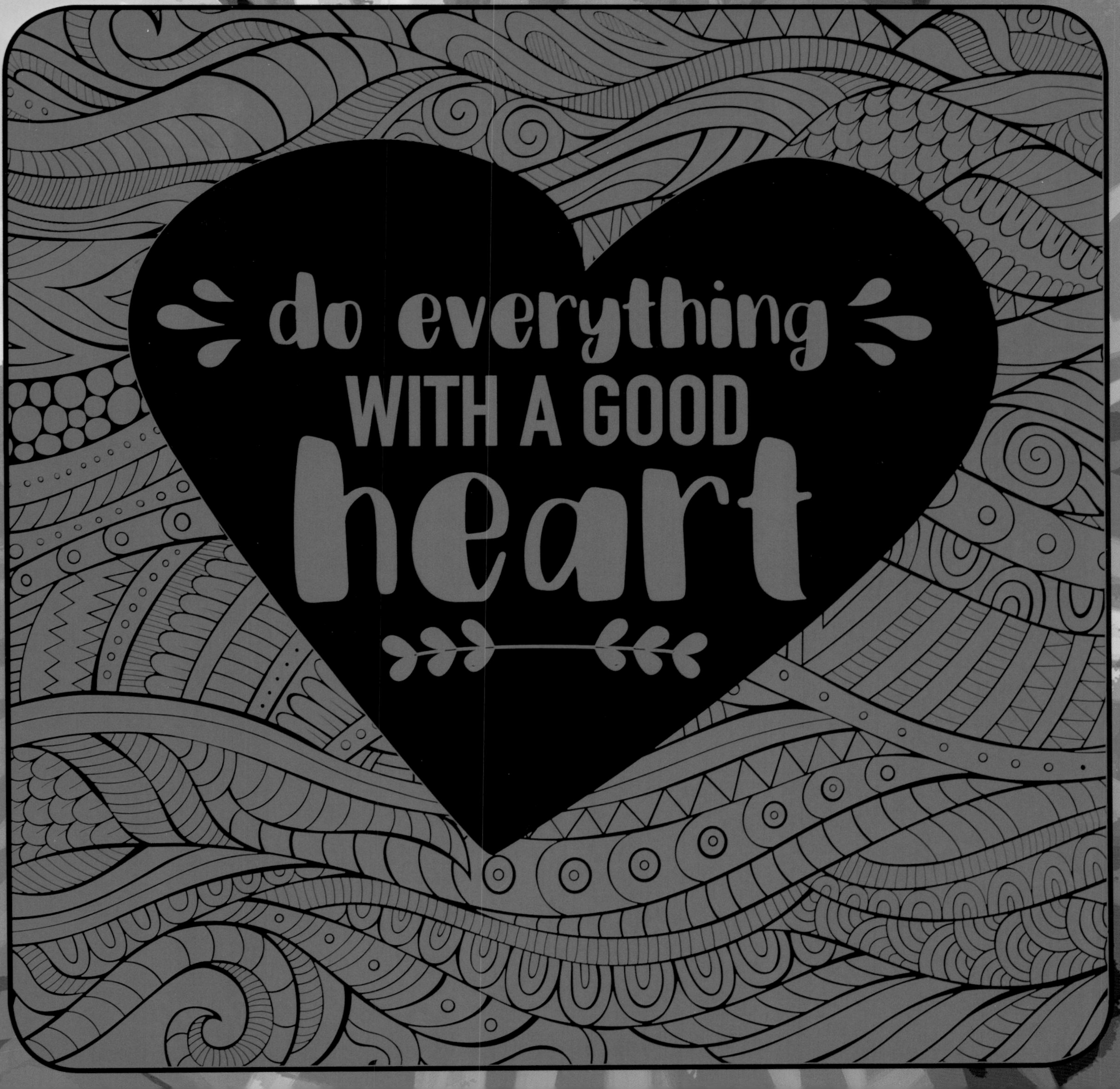
do everything
WITH A GOOD
heart

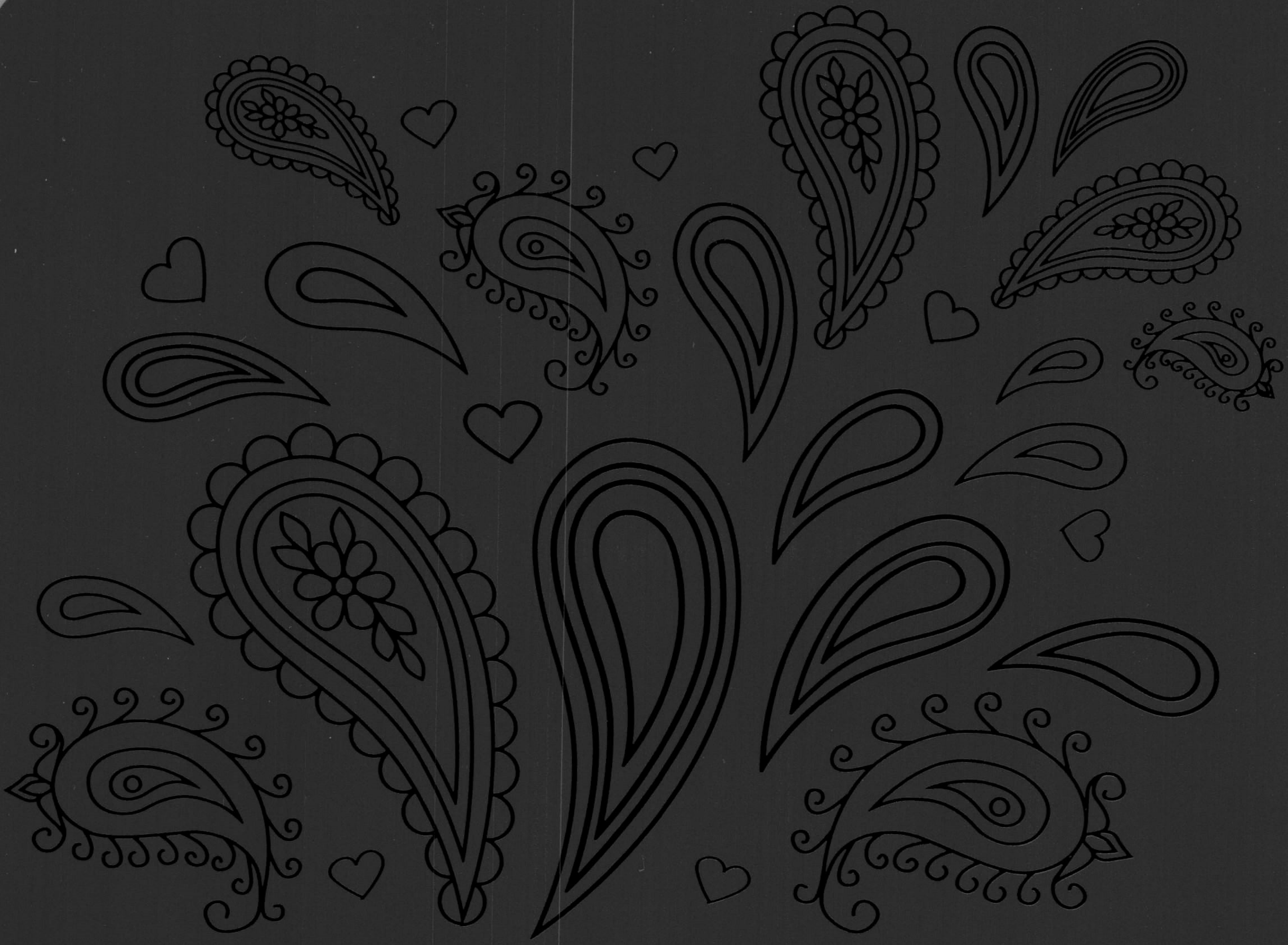

WE FALL IN LOVE BY CHANCE

We stay in love by choice

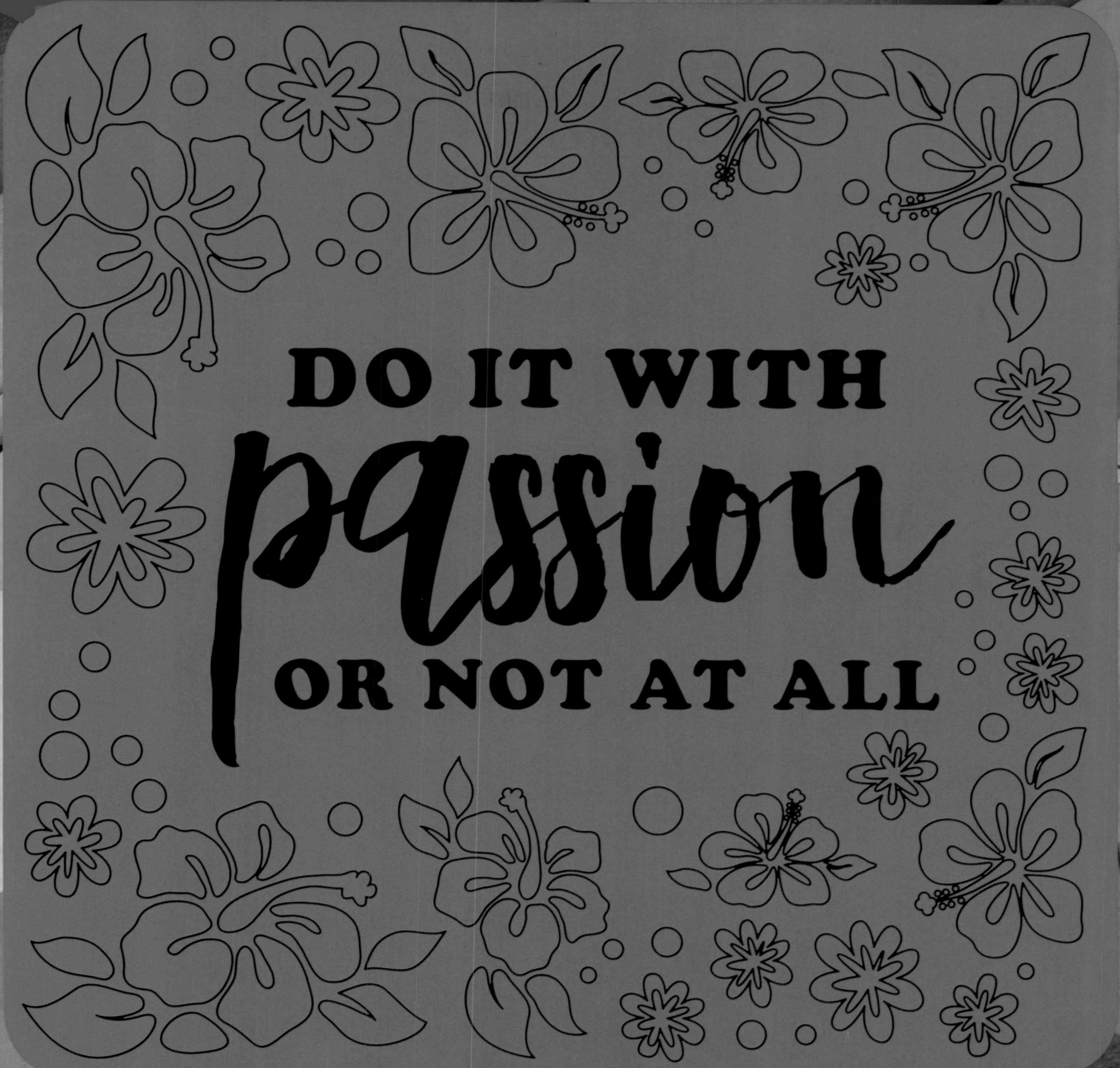
DO IT WITH
passion
OR NOT AT ALL

Being DEEPLY LOVED BY SOMEONE gives you STRENGTH WHILE LOVING SOMEONE DEEPLY gives you COURAGE

Lao Tzu

so cool